The Face of

AUSTRALIA

DAVID EVANS

Swimming Hole, Mossman Gorge, Qld

Sydney Harbour Bridge, NSW

JEFFEREYS St.

Little Hellfire Bay, Cape Le Grand National Park, WA

Edeowie, Flinders Ranges, SA

Hopetoun Falls, Otway Ranges, Vic.

The Hazards, Coles Bay, Tas.

Matilda Bay, Perth, WA

Upper Wentworth Falls, Blue, Mountains, , NSW

Geographe Bay, WA

Hamelin Bay, South West WA

Finke Gorge National Park, NT

Fig Tree, Wooroonooran, National Park, Qld

The Devils Marbles at Dusk, NT

Picadilly Valley, Adelaide Hills, SA

Cradle Mountain & Dove Lake, Tas.

Millaa Millaa Falls, Atherton Tableland, Qld

Yarra Valley, Vic.

The Granites, Lacepede Bay, SA

Ormiston Gorge, West MacDonnell Ranges, NT

Kata Tjuta – The Olgas, NT

Lucky Bay, Cape Le Grand National Park, WA

Natural Bridge, Springbrook National Park, Qld

Murray River near Mannum, SA

Boranup Karri Forest, WA

Mt Anne House, Cradle Mountain, Tas.

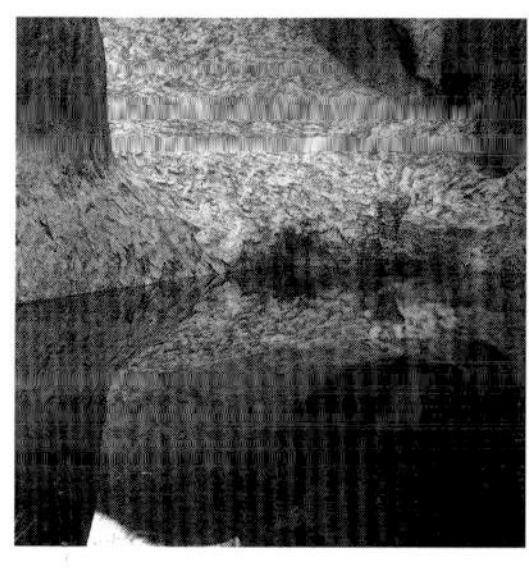

Mutitjulu Waterhole, Uluru – Ayers Rock, NT

Badger Creek, Yarra Valley, Vic.

Busselton Jetty, WA

Rainbow Valley, NT

Nandroya Falls, Wooroonooran National Park, Qld

Port Sorell, Tas.

Kings Canyon, NT

Daintree Waterhole, Qld

Cape Le Grand Sunset, WA

Palm Grove, Tamborine National Park, Qld

Pebbly Beach, Crescent Head, NSW

Kantju Gorge Waterhole, Uluru – Ayers Rock, NT

Wilpena Pound, Flinders Ranges, SA

Pandani Grove, Mt Field National Park, Tas.

Sugarloaf Rock, Leeuwin-Naturaliste National Park, WA

Russell Falls, Mt Field National Park, Tas.

Uluru – Ayers Rock, NT

Quindalup Boat Ramp, Geographe Bay, WA

Stony Rise, Little Dip Conservation Park, SA

The Twelve Apostles, Port Campbell National Park, Vic.

Mossman River, Mossman Gorge, Qld

Kata Tjuta Dusk, NT

INDEX

Apostles, Port Campbell National Park, Vic. *title page*
Badger Creek, Yarra Valley, Vic. 55
Boranup Karri Forest, WA 49
Busselton Jetty, WA 57
Cape Le Grand Sunset, WA 69
Cradle Mountain & Dove Lake, Tas. 31
Daintree Waterhole, Qld 67
The Devils Marbles at Dusk, NT 27
Edeowie, Flinders Ranges, SA 9
Fig Tree, Wooroonooran National Park, Qld 25
Finke Gorge National Park, NT 23
Geographe Bay, WA *back cover,* 19
The Granites, Lacepede Bay, SA 37
Hamelin Bay, South West WA 21
The Hazards, Coles Bay, Tas. 13
Hopetoun Falls, Otway Ranges, Vic. 11
Kantju Gorge Waterhole, Uluru – Ayers Rock, NT 75
Kata Tjuta – The Olgas, NT 41
Kata Tjuta Dusk, NT 95
Kings Canyon, NT 65
Little Hellfire Bay, Cape Le Grand National Park, WA 7
Lucky Bay, Cape Le Grand National Park, WA 43
Matilda Bay, Perth, WA 15
Millaa Millaa Falls, Atherton Tableland, Qld 33
Mossman River, Mossman Gorge, Qld 93
Mt Anne House, Cradle Mountain, Tas. 51
Murray River near Mannum, SA 47
Mutitjulu Waterhole, Uluru – Ayers Rock, NT 53
Nandroya Falls, Wooroonooran National Park, Qld 61
Natural Bridge, Springbrook National Park, Qld 45
Ormiston Gorge, West MacDonnell Ranges, NT 39
Palm Grove, Tamborine National Park, Qld 71
Pandani Grove, Mt Field National Park, Tas. 79
Pebbly Beach, Crescent Head, NSW 73
Picadilly Valley, Adelaide Hills, SA 29
Port Sorell, Tas. 63
Quindalup Boat Ramp, Geographe Bay, WA 87
Rainbow Valley, NT 59
Russell Falls, Mt Field National Park, Tas. 83
Stony Rise, Little Dip Conservation Park, SA 89
Sugarloaf Rock, Leeuwin-Naturaliste National Park, WA 81
Swimming Hole, Mossman Gorge, Qld 3
Sydney Harbour Bridge, NSW 5
The Twelve Apostles, Port Campbell National Park, Vic. 91
Uluru – Ayers Rock, NT 85
Uluru at Sunset, NT *front cover*
Upper Wentworth Falls, Blue Mountains, NSW 17
Wilpena Pound, Flinders Ranges, SA 77
Yarra Valley, Vic. 35